THE CONCISE

Coping WITH Boys

Illust

D1355179

Scholastic Children's Books,
Commonwealth House, 1-19 New Oxford Street,
London WC1A 1NU, UK
a division of Scholastic Ltd
London ~ New York ~ Toronto ~ Sydney ~ Auckland
Mexico City ~ New Delhi ~ Hong Kong

First published in the UK by Scholastic Ltd, 1992
Published in this version by Scholastic Ltd, 2000

Text copyright © Peter Corey and Kara May, 1992
Illustrations copyright © Martin Brown, 1992

ISBN 0 439 99881 6

Printed by Leo Paper Products, China

10 9 8 7 6 5 4 3 2 1

The right of Peter Corey, Kara May and Martin Brown to be identified as
the authors and illustrator of this work respectively has been asserted by
them in accordance with the Copyright, Designs and Patents Act, 1988.

Foreword

Boys, please note: you are now
approaching the half of the book
reserved for girls only. I strongly
recommend that you get back to
your own half and start reading.
And on behalf of girls everywhere,
I sincerely hope that you manage
to find new ways to cope with us.

Strictly for girls

OK, girls. That's got rid of the boys. They don't know it, but you and I know that Number 1 on our list of Talking Points isn't homework or how tigers got their spots but BOYS. So let's start talking...

Boys v. Girls

Since history began it's been Boys v. Girls, ie The (mostly) Fair Sex v. The (mostly) Foul. Battles come and go but the Battle of the Sexes goes on and on. So for starters, carry this book with you at all times. You never know when a boy might turn up.

Being a girl

Until not so long ago girls were expected to be little women, ie to stay at home and cook and sew and flit with a feather duster. If a girl wanted to do something like join the army, she ran the danger of being burnt at the stake – look at Joan of Arc! Being a girl today is far from easy. But it's a lot better than it used to be. No one's going to use you as extra kindling for the bonfire.

In the beginning...

God made a man called Adam, who bore a strong resemblance to an ape. "He's my first attempt," thought God. "I'll have another go." The next human he made was a woman. Her body was nice and curvy, she had no horrible hair on her face and her knees weren't knobbly. "I have to say, Adam, she's a definite improvement on you." And nothing's changed since.

What is a boy?

So that we know what to avoid, we must first decide what a boy is. Rumour has it that boys are made of the following ingredients:

slugs
snails
puppy dogs' tails

which explains their unruly, slimy behaviour. The problem with boys is that they can't decide what they are. I've seen little boys at kindergarten strutting round the playground like men. And I've seen grown men with paunches running round the football pitch on a Sunday afternoon, in the mistaken belief that they're still young boys. Nobody knows exactly what a boy is, but I shall attempt to identify some boy types and where you'll find them.

The yob

He's flashy, dressy and a loudmouth. You'll find him showing off his tonsils on the football terraces. But underneath, he's a real softie. You could wrap him round your little finger – but would you want to? He eats with his mouth open, belches loudly and won't get on with your parents. But that could be a good thing.

Chat-up line: "Oi! You!"

The brain box

Also known as the egg-head owing
to the shape of his head. He thinks
a lot and thinks that thinking is the
most important thing you can do.
You'll find him in the school library
with his nose stuck in a big book.

Chat-up line: "I'm a genius."

The good-looking guy

Wow! It's not just the teeth! It's the tan, it's the eyes, it's everything about him. But how do you find him? Join the crowd of girls outside the school gates. He'll be in the middle of it somewhere.

Chat-up line: He doesn't need one. With his looks, girls fall at his feet and he picks up the one he likes best.

The New Age Greenie

See the boy standing in the pouring rain holding a "Save the Whale" poster? That's the Greenie. Recycles other boys' old socks and jeans by buying clothes at Oxfam. Doesn't eat cows or other animals. If it's romance you want, forget it. He saves all his energy for saving endangered species.

Chat-up line: "Would you like a leaf of my lettuce?"

The Hulk

He's the Tarzan/Rambo lookalike.
This chunky lad is living proof of
Darwin's theory of evolution, that
man is descended from the ape.
You'll find him in the school gym,
swinging on a rope. The Hulk is a
big boy with a small brain.

Chat-up line: "Grunt! Grunt! Grunt!"

Knight in Shining Armour

Incredibly handsome, polite, charming, strong, brave, adventurous. Gives his life for your slightest whim, likes everything you like, admires you more than any girl in the world and you can meet him in daydreams and fairy tales. He's perfect, BUT ... in the real world he doesn't exist.

Chat-up line: "Your wish is my command."

The Wimp

The Wimp bleats rather than speaks, blames others, never himself, and is always on the lookout for a shoulder to cry on. You'll find him on top of his desk when the school hamster escapes or at home, tied to his mum's apron strings.

Chat-up line: "Er, er, er..."

The Nice Guy

He smiles a lot, sincerely, and is sincerely interested in what you say, even if it's boring. (You can't be fascinating all the time.) He's the one type of boy who'll borrow your biro and give it back and who'll help his kid sister with her homework. The trouble is, nice guys are like flannels ... wet.

Chat-up line: "I think Robbie Williams is brill, don't you?"

A guide to coping

Now we know what boys are (sort of), what they're made of and the types they come in. But how do we cope with them? I'm hoping that what follows will help you to avoid the pitfalls a lot of us girls have stumbled into. Good luck! I hope you cope better than I did!

The "aaah!" factor

When a boy makes you go "aaah!"
it's for one of three reasons:

1 He's revolting.
2 He's gorgeous.
3 He's trodden on your foot.

If he's revolting, don't give him a
second look. If he's gorgeous,
remember beauty is only skin deep.
And if it's your foot he's trodden
on, tread on his.

Acne

He's got acne. In case it's escaped
his notice, should you point out to
him his face is a minefield of
flaming spots? Not unless you want
to be clobbered with insults. Never
come between a boy and his acne.
Let them sort it out between them.

Adolescent

The adolescent boy is one of the most disruptive and tiresome species to set his clumsy feet upon the planet. In our society adolescent boys are allowed to roam free causing havoc and mayhem. There's only one person who can get them under control – the adolescent girl.

Aggro

A boy who never causes you aggro (aggravation) is a rare specimen, if not unique. If you come across one, parcel him up and send him to the Natural History Museum, where they'll put him in a glass case and preserve him for posterity.

Brother (your own)

Your brother is not something you have a choice about. He's inflicted on you by your parents. Brothers operate in the belief that they're sent into the world to cause sisters aggravation. Like reading your diary out in the school playground. Don't be tempted to cause a scene. As the old saying goes, revenge is a dish best eaten cold. One day he'll bring a girlfriend home...

Brother (your friend's)

They are rarely as aggravating as your own. Some of them may be worthy of your friendship or even something deeper...

BROTHERS

YOURS

SOMEONE ELSE'S

Dates (edible)

They're a dark brown, sticky fruit,
usually eaten at Christmas,
stuffed. They should not be
confused with the inedible variety
(see opposite).

Dates (inedible, with boys)

In common with the edible variety, a date with a boy can leave you wondering why you bothered. On the other hand, it can be surprisingly enjoyable. Alas, there's no way of telling how things are going to turn out: the date that you think is going to be sheer heaven can turn into a nightmare, while the date you're dreading can turn out to be unadulterated bliss.

Ego

A boy's ego is the part of him he likes best. His ego not only tells him how remarkable (clever, handsome, etc) he is, it tells the rest of the world as well. A boy with a big ego is filled with admiration for himself and will expect equally unstinting admiration from you.

Embarrassment

First the bad news: at some time or other a boy will cause you embarrassment – it's an experience no girl escapes. The good news is that it's one of the worst experiences you'll ever have to go through, and you'll survive! No girl has actually died of embarrassment ... so far.

Feelings

Tell him you're feeling hurt because
he forgot your birthday and he'll
look at you as if you're seriously
sick and suggest you see a doctor.
Because boys don't have feelings,
they'll try to make out there's
something wrong with you if
you have any.

Frog

When a male frog is kissed by a princess, it turns into a prince. If you're a princess, go get yourself a fishing net, catch yourself a frog and press your lips to his. If you're not a princess, kissing frogs isn't recommended.

Jokes

What a boy thinks of as a funny joke (Ha, Ha!) may not make you laugh. It may make you feel sick or nothing at all. When this happens never fake a laugh. It will only encourage him to tell another sick/unfunny joke.

Kissing

As boys get older, they develop a keen interest in kissing, so watch out! They'll kiss any girl they can lay their hands on. Some boys' kisses land on your cheek neatly. Others have no sense of direction and a kiss meant for you goes smack! on the tree behind you. Kissing is like playing the violin – it improves with practice. Tell him to buy himself a violin and practise on that.

Muscles

A boy who is proud of his muscles (lumpy, bulging shapes on arms, chest and legs) rarely has anything else to be proud of, like a brain. He longs for the return of the Cave Age, when brawn not brains was best and the brawny boy with bulging muscles was much in demand for wielding a stone club.

Rat

The male rat is often a strikingly handsome and deceptively charming guy, who flatters you to your face and insults you behind your back. Never give a rat a second chance. Once a rat, always a rat. Give him the boot NOW!

Wally

Some boys are born Wallies. Your modern Wally stays up all night doing his homework, then leaves it on the bus so he has to stay in and do it all again. But think twice before you dump a Wally. His heart is in the right place and he'll always put you first.

STOP!
On no account move past this point.

You don't really want to know what any stupid boys think, do you? Oh, you do? Well, alright then...

Turn the book around until it's upside down. Now close the book and start reading "Coping with Girls". Better still, read the full version of this half in "Coping with Boys".

Ex

How you feel about your ex-boyfriend depends on how you parted. Did he jump or was he pushed? If you gave him the push you may still want him for a friend. If he jumped, you're more likely to want his head served up on a plate with an apple in his mouth.

Yawn

A wide opening of the mouth left uncovered by boys who are under the illusion that you want to look at their tonsils.

STOP!
On no account move past this point.

Oh, all right then, if you must –
but watch out, you do so at
your own risk!

Turn the book round until it's
upside down. Now close the book
and start reading "Coping with
Boys". Better still, read the full
version of this half in "Coping
with Girls".

Youthclubs

Youthclubs, in fact clubs of all descriptions, are great places to meet girls (except boys' clubs). Mainly because you are under no pressure. If you want to chat to girls, then you can. Just one word of warning, if you go with your friends. A bunch of lads all trying to impress a bunch of girls often has the opposite effect. So be warned, lads!

X-girlfriend

This refers to any girl who was once the object of your affections, but no longer is. It may dent your ego to learn that girls probably cope with becoming an ex better than boys. You see, girls generally get more attention from the opposite sex than boys do. And that attention can be a great morale-booster when you're on the rebound.

Teasing

Some boys may tell you that the way to get a girl to notice you is to tease her. And it just might work. But it might also get you thumped, because teasing is very cruel. Of course if you get thumped you learn all about teasing: "Thumped by a girl? Ha!" The lads will have a tease-a-thon!

Romance

Blokes aren't really supposed to be romantic, are they? I mean, if we start making these little romantic gestures, won't everyone think we've gone a bit funny? The answer is this: if you feel the need to make a romantic gesture towards a female, don't fight it – but be prepared for your mates to take the mickey for the next ten years.

A SIMPLE PASS

Passes

If you're thinking, "Oh, I've got one of them! For the bus!", then I would hazard a guess that you are about as far away from coping with girls as anyone could ever be. I am referring to the means by which people indicate they are interested in each other. Passes can include all sorts of little looks, winks, nudges and note-swapping.

Over-enthusiasm

In any dealings with the opposite sex, over-enthusiasm is a complete non-starter. It just doesn't work. You need to remain aloof in affairs of the heart. Girls do not like to be rushed for any reason. So the key is ... be cool.

Love

Billions upon billions of words have
been written about love. Entire rain
forests have been sacrificed on
the altar of love. But no one has
ever really defined what it is. And
this book is no exception.

Kissing

This is a difficult one, isn't it? It is always fraught with "Should I?", "Shouldn't I?", "What will she say?" etc etc etc. Everything depends on whether or not she actually wants you to kiss her, doesn't it? So be careful. When you look into her eyes and see that far-away look, make sure it really is The Moment, and not just the fact that she's forgotten to put in her contact lenses!

Jealousy

Jealousy is poisonous. Avoid it. You see everyone as a rival for your girlfriend's affections. And I mean everyone. Even your best mate. Jealousy has killed more friendships than almost anything else. And if you want to hold on to the love of your life, then beware jealousy!

SWOON
SWOON

Glasses

Someone once said, "Men don't make passes at girls who wear glasses." But do girls make passes at men who wear glasses? Well, it does seem that a pair of "specs" is no longer the barrier it once used to be to finding yourself attractive to girls. Modern specs are really very trendy – they might even be cool (whatever that is).

Gifts

There comes a time in every young man's life when he feels the overwhelming urge to buy a female a present. Unfortunately, choosing the right kind of present to give to a girl is a minefield. Good gifts: sweets or chocolates, flowers, anything expensive. Bad gifts: socks, wrestling magazine, deodorant.

Flirting

Look up "flirting" in a dictionary
and you'll discover that it means
"wooing frivolously". You'll discover
that flirting is something that
girls enjoy, so you'll have to be able
to tell the difference between
flirting and serious attraction,
otherwise it could all end in tears.
Yours, probably.

Disco

Traditionally, a great place to meet girls. It's also a great place to dance with girls, as long as you don't mind dancing with their five mates and their handbags. It is not, however, a good place to talk to girls unless you have a voice like a foghorn.

Acne

It's a sad fact (but true) that there comes a time in every young man's life when his face breaks out in terrible spots. This happens about the same time as you notice that girls are quite interesting. There's nothing you can do about it. And it's little consolation to learn that girls suffer from it too.

A guide to coping

Now we know what girls are (sort of), what they're made of and the types they come in. But how do we cope with them? I'm hoping that what follows will help you to avoid the pitfalls a lot of us boys have stumbled into. Good luck! I hope you cope better than I did!

The Limpet

These girls appear to be magnetically attached to you. Even if you are in separate rooms, houses or towns, you can feel them looking longingly at you. Hear them sigh every time you move your elbow.

The Spy

To be found wherever they shouldn't be when you least want them there. If they are also your little sister, this makes them doubly deadly. They mean to cause you as much trouble as they possibly can, and it's easy to imagine that they're in the pay of your parents.

The Go-Between

Every class has one. And if you suddenly find that you have a passion for a girl in your class, but don't know how to tell her, this is the girl to go to. Come wind, hail or driving blizzard, she will get the message through! Unfortunately, she'll often give the message to the rest of the class too.

The Know-All

To be found at the top of the class, at the front of the race, on the platform of the school debating society. In fact, anywhere where there's a chance to be first. For she's that scary thing, a Very Intelligent Female. And boy, does she know it!

The Groupie

You'll find her on the touchline at every school sporting event, seemingly the team's biggest fan. But listen carefully to her cheers. Don't they sound more like jeers? You can only hope that one day she'll stop turning up to matches because she's found herself a boyfriend.

The Raving Beauty

She is the subject of fantasies, fictions, boasts and brawls and she is completely inaccessible. She's so beautiful that no boy ever dares speak to her. You can never get to know this particular type of girl apart from in your dreams and even then she'll ignore you.

The Tomboy

Any lad who ever had a gang has met the tomboy. There's one in every gang. The good thing about having a tomboy in your gang is that when you go off torturing frogs and on to torturing girls, you've got one to practise on.

What is a girl?

"Sugar and spice and all things nice. That's what little girls are made of." Whoever said that, has obviously never bitten one. But what are they? Are they human? Where do they come from? How soon can they be sent back there? I'm going to run through a few girl types, but believe me, there are more weird girls out there than I could ever fit into this tiny book...

In the beginning...

God created Man in his own image and called him Adam, a name that never really caught on. Then, while Adam was asleep, God borrowed one of his ribs and created Eve. And there we have it in a nutshell, the reason why everything's gone wrong ever since. Adam was asleep. If he'd been awake, he could have told God not to make him a woman – a Scalextric would be fine. But that's how it all started.

Being a boy

It's not easy being a boy. Being a boy is tough because, even from a very early age, a great deal is expected of you. Dads want you to play for your national football team and mums want you to show your sensitive side. It's just not fair. But you have to grin and bear it. Preferably a stupid inane grin that will convince your parents you're insane and should be left well alone.

The Battle of the Sexes

This isn't a battle, it's war. And although it may be impossible for us to win, chaps, I hope that with the aid of this book you might be able to come second equal. So read, learn and inwardly digest. But don't reveal the secrets contained in these pages to a GIRL! After all, they are the enemy.

Think back...

Just to prove my point, think back
to when you were very small. Who
was it who used to tell you what to
do? Your mum. When you started
school, who was it who told you to
get up? Mum! That woman again.
Who decided what you wear? Not
your dad, that's for sure. The
pattern is set from childhood –
women are in control.

Strictly for boys

I shall now assume that I am addressing myself exclusively to chaps, males, blokes, lads, boyos etc. Coping with girls is hard enough, without them finding out how we do it! That would give them an unfair advantage and personally, I think they've got that already.

Foreword

I think I should say straight away that if you're a girl reading this, you've probably got the book the wrong way round. I'll give you a second to check. Done it? Good. NOW, BOG OFF!